THIS IS LIFE

Real Stories from the Road

THIS IS LIFE

Real Stories from the Road

BOB LENZ

THIS IS LIFE
Real Stories from the Road

First Edition, June 2012

Published by Life Press

www.lifepromotions.com

Author Services by Pedernales Publishing, LLC.
www.pedernalespublishing.com

ISBN 978-0-9856716-0-0

Printed in the United States of America

Dedication

To anyone who has ever felt an emptiness that lingers, even after the heights of success.

To anyone who has ever experienced the darkness of despair and defeat and the depths of loneliness in your heart.

To all the youth who have ever felt like they didn't matter...

May the words of these pages and the love of Jesus convince you that you do matter, and that God is the God of the mountaintops and the valleys.

Contents

Appreciation

I'd like to thank my wife, Carol, for sharing life with me. It's been an amazing adventure. I'd also like to thank her for sharing me with others as I travel, so that others may know and find the source of life. I'd like to thank Tammy, my assistant, who takes my chicken scratches and rambling rabbit trails and puts them down into ink to truly convey what my heart and head wants to say. Thanks for co-writing this and still putting my name on the cover.

INTRODUCTION

I love a good story. I think everyone does. But something happens inside me when the cover of a book or the opening screen of a movie says, "Based on a true story." It grabs the emotions of my heart a little stronger. It seems so much more intense. This really happened to someone? To them? It may cause my heart to bleed with sorrow because of a real-life tragedy, or explode with joy over a happy ending. I try to imagine those circumstances happening to me and the story suddenly becomes more personal, more compelling, more captivating.

So let me assure you at the beginning of this book that all the stories are real. They're true. They are not made up. Instead, these are stories of real lives, real hurts, real joys, real dreams and real people I've met as I've traveled back roads and byways across the country.

I've shared these stories with others through the years and have often been asked to compile them. That's how this book came about. I share them with you in the hope that it will encourage, challenge and increase your faith in a big God who can bring good out of pain and still change lives. Even yours.

I wish I could tell you that every story has a happy ending or closure, but I remind you that all my stories are true, and that's just not how real life works. We live in a fallen world. Along with joys and triumphs, life encounters many hurts and heartaches along the way. But my prayer and hope is that those stories will increase our awareness of what people are going through. Maybe as a result we will join the cause of bringing hope and life to young and old alike.

And we know from scripture that true life comes from the giver of life himself. For this is life... to know You. (John 17:3)

THIS IS LIFE

Real Stories from the Road

In the Beginning

THERE WERE LOTS OF BIBLE STUDIES, worship times, campfires, testimonies and training. There were no hotels, not even camp cabins. The small group all camped out in tents. As predicted, it rained one night, but the students ate it up.

As time went by they began sharing about their friends and how they wanted them to know Christ. A passion was stirring and they began realizing that the best thing they could ever do is share Jesus with their friends.

It was a discipleship camp for only 30 campers. It was a small event for youth who were leaders, an encouragement to go deeper in their faith, to train and equip them to make a difference in their school campuses by instilling a passion for evangelism. It was an event to teach them to see with eternal eyes, a time not only to learn to resist temptation, but a time to get m.a.d. – *make a difference*.

Together, they discussed strategies of how to reach their friends, or maybe a whole class. Then people began to have visions of how they could reach their whole school for Christ. In fact, why not reach the whole state and allow every student, in a relational setting, to hear a clear and personal presentation of the Gospel. It's the true story of a personal Jesus who loves them and wants to spend eternity with them and wants to impact their world so they can make a difference in the lives of their friends and school.

Then someone posed the question, "Why just our state? Let's reach our country so that the people we reach can reach the world for Christ."

Then a loud and boisterous 17-year-old kid stood to his feet. I knew this kid. I knew he wasn't even walking strong in his faith. He was compromising his values and drinking a lot in high school, among other offenses. But as he stood to his feet he was compelled to yell out, "Yeah, let's do it! Let's reach all 50 states!"

In their zeal, the students began drafting up a covenant that stated, "We, the undersigned, vow to commit our lives to Jesus and pledge to allow God to use us to reach our friends, campuses, state and country – all 50 states for the gospel. We vow to link our arms with others in love, that they would know who we serve and that we are His disciples."

All 30 signed it. As they did, the speaker thought, maybe it was worth the time and effort after all, even if it was just for 30 kids.

I'm so glad that he and God felt it was worth it. Why? Because this story is about me.

No, I wasn't the speaker! I was that boisterous 17-year-old kid who yelled, "Yeah, let's reach all 50 states!"

I answered the call that day when I was 17 years old in June of 1980 and sincerely said, "God I want to share about you and your love in all 50 states." So 28 years later on May 21, 2008, I spoke in Saco, Maine – the last of the 50 states.

Ironically, 30 youth received Christ as their savior that night. It's so humbling that God honored a 17-year-old's prayer, and that by God's grace he has allowed me to be used to lead people to Christ in all 50 states. He truly has done infinitely more than I could have ever dared to ask or imagine (Ephesians 3:20).

UPDATE: I read over this story again before putting it in this book. It's been three years since I originally wrote it. It seems wild because I was just in Los Angeles at a convention with the National Network of Youth Ministries where 60 leaders from around the country were gathered. They were from various denominations representing different organizations like Youth for Christ, Youth Specialties, Simply Youth and Every Campus...some of the largest youth ministries in the nation. While gathered, we signed another covenant stating that all of us in youth ministry would link arms together to reach every student before the age of 18. So, as I read this story again, it felt like God's timing that I had just signed another covenant containing the same commitment I made as a 17-year-old. It made me feel like that teenager all over again.

PRAYER

Renew the vigor and passion of my youth. Never let the fire in my bones die out. Use me to reach the world for your glory.

Looking for Love

"I'M ONE WHO NEVER FIT IN," she said. These words came from a girl I talked with in Pennsylvania where I spoke not long ago. "I'm teased and have had rocks thrown at me," she continued. "I was raped and have to deal with physical, emotional and verbal abuse. I had my fingers bent backwards and was knocked unconscious. I don't understand. I'm a nice person. And I try to be very kind to everyone. I just wanted to be treated with some measure of humanity... some measure of decency. I don't fit in anywhere. Home. School. Don't they know I still have a heart? I still do, you know."

I couldn't believe my ears as I listened to her. Then she told me she never believed in God because she couldn't understand how he could let all these bad things happen to her.

So she searched for love in the arms of the opposite sex. It was something that made her feel wanted, cherished and held. Do you see why the intimacy of sex, even for a night, would seem so appealing to her? She maybe even convinced herself that it really was love. But when her boyfriend broke up with her she started cutting. It all culminated with a suicide attempt the week before I came to her school.

She mentioned that she had been at a party over the weekend where the conversation of why bad things happen to people came up again. She recalled someone saying, "I don't know why it happens, but I know God is big enough and can turn something so *[expletive]* into something beautiful. Because God is love, and that's not his purpose."

The party where these stirring words were spoken was on the weekend. Only a few days later she heard me at her school sharing another message of hope: that no matter what people have done, whether they've abused you, used you or abandoned you, you still have value.

She was intrigued enough to come back in the evening for an evangelistic rally where she told me this story, her story, while we were sharing pizza after the program.

I looked at her and asked, "Where are you now with the whole God thing?" She replied, "I know there has to be something or someone out there somewhere."

Her tone changed slightly as she went on, "It's just like your talk said, Bob... I'm looking for love. I'm just looking for love." She lowered her head, unable to look up.

I reached out and lifted her chin to have her look at me. "Did you raise your hand tonight?" I asked.

With tears now rolling down her cheeks she said, "Yes. Yes, I did." I asked her why. She simply responded, "I guess I believe. I guess I do believe in Jesus after all."

End of story.

Actually not. I think it's just the beginning of a new story. Pray that she stays connected with a local faith community. Someone from the church who brought us in has followed up with her so she can grow in her new relationship with God and have a network of people who can help her through the pains and hurts of life.

Her search for true love has come true by knowing love Himself. God is love. Jesus, His son who has come, is love. And they are now in a relationship.

PRAYER

Forgive me for pursuing fulfillment outside of you. Draw me back to the one love that never fails. Help me to not judge people by their actions, but to see through to their heart which is so desperately crying out, looking for love.

I Lost a Junior High Kid

I SUSPECT THAT EVERY PARENT can remember the moment and knows the emotion of being in a crowded area, suddenly realizing that you don't know where your child is. Ours was at Disneyland when our kids were small. My son, David, disappeared. It was only five minutes, but it was among the most agonizing five minutes of my life, filled with fear, panic and despair.

My mind raced with irrational thoughts of my son wandering away and falling into the moat surrounding Sleeping Beauty's castle, or worse, a sinister child predator lurking in the shadows, waiting to lure him away. We desperately asked passers-by, "Have you seen a little boy with curly hair?" We frantically searched everywhere, calling out his name, "David! David!"

Finally, we found him, and our hearts were overwhelmed with gratitude as tears streamed down our faces and we held him, never wanting to let go again.

I can't imagine the agony of parents who never find their child again. Have you, like me, recalled seeing photos of lost children displayed at Walmart, or others that were pictured on the backs of milk cartons? I can't even allow my mind to think what it would be like if those photos were of one of my own children.

During those five minutes of panic and fear, I was willing to do anything, talk to anyone and get anyone's attention, because I feared my son was gone.

It makes me wonder: do we really believe that a student without Christ is lost? If so, where is the panic? Where is the emotion? Where is the urgency to find them? Do we believe their life is in danger, that their very soul is at stake, and that their only hope of being found is in jeopardy?

If we really believed they were falling into the hands of a sinister enemy, wouldn't we do anything? Wouldn't we do whatever it takes to find them?

The reality is we are losing kids every day. Statistics tell us that only about 18% of our nation's youth are in the safety of a church family,[1] and if we don't reach them before the age of 18, their chances of coming to faith in Christ are significantly less. In fact, the latest research indicates that our best chance of reaching them is before the age of 14.[2]

Yes, 14. That's junior high.

I recently returned from Kansas where I spoke at my first school assembly program of the school year. Bethany, a junior in high school, heard me at a conference, and she wanted her friends to hear me too. Something stirred her heart and awakened the realization that she was surrounded by a mission field ready for the harvest. She wanted her friends who were lost to be found; to know Jesus. So she arranged to have me come to her community.

I spoke at Bethany's school last week, and our team at Life Promotions worked with her to host a rally the same evening where I could share the gospel. Many of the junior and senior high students who heard me during the day returned for the evening program, and because of Bethany's diligence, 50 kids responded to the gospel and were taken back from the enemy. Their photos are no longer displayed on the enemy's bulletin board; instead, their names are written in the Book of Life.

Bethany felt the overwhelming need to reach her friends, and was willing to do whatever it took. Her overwhelming desperation to reach her friends was replaced with overwhelming joy at seeing so many of them come to Christ.

While on my sabbatical, God made it clear to me that I was not done. There are many more who need the hope of Christ. I've been in ministry now for nearly 30 years, but I feel God has made it clear that the greatest years are still ahead.

I decided that if I have a lot of years to go, then I'm going to have to take better care of myself, so I began exercising and watching my diet. I've now lost 75 pounds, which is ironically the total weight of some of those junior high kids I just spoke to. I'll gladly lose more weight, but I never want to lose another junior high kid.

God has many more opportunities in store to reach out to this generation and call their hearts back to Christ, back to their parents, and to the Creator of their souls.

Jesus said He came to seek and save the lost. He left a lot. He gave a lot. He sacrificed all. Why? To see one lost sheep saved.

PRAYER

God, make me desperate for others to know you. Fill my heart with a passion to seek out the lost and hurting. Fill me with holy discontent.

The Determination of One

THANKFULLY, THE SUN WAS STARTING TO SET, bringing the temperature beneath 100 degrees. I was speaking at Creation Northwest festival when it was held at the Gorge, a beautiful natural amphitheater overlooking a vast canyon and a beautiful river in Washington State. There were over 20,000 people in attendance.

It was the third year in a row that I had spoken at this event. The talk I gave was titled "Hitler Was Wrong," validating the worth of every person. I taught on how T4 was the address where scientists did experiments on people they deemed to be less than human. The victims endured unheard-of torture and cruelty. Hitler and those at T4 developed a propaganda campaign known as *Life Not Worthy of Life*. It diminished the value of the handicapped, elderly, and eventually led to the extermination of Jews and other people groups.

Through God's word we built a case: because of the cross every person has value and is called to fight against this ludicrous philosophy and the core of it that is still prevalent in our society today. We esteem some higher than others because of external features, appearance and abilities. It's a philosophy that, at its core, is not much different than the philosophy held by Hitler.

Perhaps it sounds extreme, but the beginning of prejudice and hatred towards others begins with a subtle feeling of superiority over those who are different. Left unchecked or challenged, it will become like an infected wound, spreading to other parts of the body.

I ended the program by inviting my handicapped sister, Lois, to join me on stage to sing *It's Good to Be Alive*. Wow, what an impact. God uses any willing vessel.

The response was tremendous, but there was one young man in particular who really impacted me. His name is Clark, a sharp-looking student who would be a senior that school year. He attended a different high school than his siblings to participate in some special needs classes. I mentioned in my talk that I was personally in one of those special needs classes for a speech impediment when I was younger, and I remember being called "retarded" like my brother, Tim and sister, Lois.

Clark was touched by God and took on the challenge of reaching his school for Christ. For two months he worked at pulling people together, trying to raise the resources, organizing dates, getting an okay from the school, and looking for a church to host the evening rally. Our office coached, encouraged and prayed with him through many ups and downs, especially when Clark was ready to give up because of how little support he received from people he tried to get on board with his idea.

But God opened the door. The first $500 of support came from the Creation Festival to aid him in the outreach. This was a catalyst for other churches and groups. They listened a little more intently when they heard Creation was sponsoring it. What a partnership we have with Creation – what Kingdom thinking.

It was all set up. It's a go. But wait, the principal said no? What!?

What a roller coaster ride of emotions. After the principal spoke with some other teachers, they discouraged him because of the unknown. They had concerns because we are a Christian organization, even though we always uphold the law and never share faith-based content in public schools. After going back and forth with reassurances and difficult conversations, the promise from the principal didn't stand. He determined that he would only allow it if it were an after-school assembly program.

Can I use the word "stupid?" Who would want to stay for a program after school? I know as a student I wouldn't have stayed. As a speaker, I didn't even want to go!

I was so frustrated, disappointed and tired, and to be truthful, I had little, if any faith. Honestly, the only reason we didn't cancel was for one simple reason: Clark and his dream. He had put so much into this. It was even going to be his senior project.

We had a band lined up to perform and I had honestly hoped for 20 people to show up, including our team and those who brought me in. To my surprise, we had 175 people come out for the program. You should have seen the excitement in Clark's eyes. That alone made it worth it. Later that evening we still scheduled an evangelistic rally not affiliated with the schools, so we hoped for maybe half as many who were at the after-school assembly to come back, which would have been about 90 people – a higher percentage than our normal return. Instead, we had 300 people come out! Of those, 47 people accepted Christ as their savior. God is so faithful, even when we're not. More important than the number of kids I hoped would show up, was that God showed up.

Turns out, the principal was at the event and did invite us to come back and speak to the whole school during the day. Testimonies came from so many people who talked to me after the program. But I thought I'd share a note from Clark's mom that tells about Clark's experience. This note should also serve as an encouragement to us as parents to not sit back and simply say, "Yes, that would be nice," in response to our children's dreams, but to have confidence and give encouragement that they truly can make a difference in their world.

"Thank you for making this dream come true for our son, Clark. He is a very determined boy who has had a tough road all through his academic career. What a way to end his senior year! It will be a memory and accomplishment he will never forget. He tries so hard but has never had the ability to achieve academically or in the sports world like his siblings, so this is huge for Clark and our whole family. Thank you from the bottom of our hearts! God bless your ministry. We will always support it."

Sometimes the impact is not just on those I speak to at an event, but for those who organize the event as well. God, who allowed a student to have a vision and a dream, also helped it to come true. Clark, way to trust God and work your butt off for your friends. The determination of one has impacted an entire community and untold others. You've made a difference! Live the rest of your life like that!

Since then, God has continued to use Clark, who has gone on to live out his faith even more by serving on mission trips and has even made a two year commitment to serve with Youth with a Mission. I'm reminded once again of His word: "Now to him who is able to do immeasurably more than all we ask or imagine, according to his power that is at work within us." – Ephesians 3:20 (NIV)

Contact Life Promotions at info@lifepromotions.com to view a video of Clark sharing about his experience.

PRAYER

God, never let me minimize who You will use and what You can do. It's by Your power, not mine.

Go Into All the World

A FRIEND ASKED ME, "Where do you live?" I jokingly replied, "My wife says I live on Delta Airlines." They laughed, but I'm not laughing as I'm sitting in a cramped airline seat again.

"A Redeye flight" seems like an appropriate name as I fly through the night, having left San Francisco at 11:00PM, unable to sleep, yet unable to stay awake either. I'm in a land somewhere in between. I will fly into Green Bay at 9:30 in the morning, where my wife, Carol, will pick me up for the first day of our vacation. Can you say "Red Bull?"

My road manager, John, and I just did some fun math. I have flown over a million miles on Delta Airlines alone. To go around the whole world is 25,046 miles (in case you were wondering). That means I have spent enough time on Delta alone to go around the world more than 40 times.

Anyone who thinks traveling is glamorous has obviously not traveled. Oh, please don't hear me complaining, but I do want you to hear my heart.

Our mission at Life Promotions is to reach as many youth as possible with the Gospel before the age of 18. We call it Mission <18> to demonstrate that we are indeed missionaries. Yet I believe we often envision missionaries as those who travel around the world to remote villages and foreign cultures to reach people with the Gospel of Jesus Christ.

We may not trek the plains of Africa, but we travel around the globe to reach a culture that does seem foreign to many: American youth. We love them with all our hearts. But more importantly, God loves them. That's why we present the Gospel in their language and their culture, so that just one more may come to know Jesus as their Lord and Savior. That's evangelism. That's the great commission. That's a mission field.

"Go into all the world..." That includes our nation, our communities, our schools, even our own backyards.

We will zigzag across this nation to team with churches, schools, music festivals, and conferences. Anywhere and any time we can get a captive audience to listen to the Good News, we want to be there.

I just spoke to 12,000 people at a festival in Monterey, California. When it came time to respond to the Gospel I gave an invitation for people to raise their hands to trust in Jesus. All I could see were hands. I had them keep them up until a follow-up person could get them information and pray with them.

They had 500 volunteers and ran out of materials. One volunteer alone prayed with over 40 people. They estimated 2,000-3,000 hands were raised to receive Christ.

I can't imagine how the angels were spilling over with joy, rejoicing in heaven, because I myself was higher than a kite.

After I spoke, I went to the prayer tent. One of the people I met was named Bill, a guy who thought God could never forgive him for a sexual sin he had committed. But that night he believed and received Jesus, and he experienced forgiveness from the High Eternal Lover.

I'm still in the air. I'm still tired. My eyes are still red. But I can't wait to fly again. Why? There are more Bill's down there, waiting to hear a message of grace, forgiveness and love. Where is your mission field?

PRAYER

Help us to remember that we are all missionaries and have a mission field, whether we share across picket fences or international borders.

I've Seen It All Before

TO BE HONEST, my heart was saying, "I've seen this all before." It wasn't even as if I was taking it lightly; it was just that I was so busy supporting a great ministry and calling others to support it or get involved, that I didn't see my own need and how God had sent me on this trip for me. I always want to do something for God, which isn't bad in itself, but I easily forget that He wants me to be in relationship with Him, the God of the universe, even more every day.

I was in El Salvador. My reason for going was to introduce some friends to the work of an awesome organization, Compassion International. I truly believe in their work, and for the last 15 years it's been a part of my ministry to students and families, to provide them an opportunity to sponsor a child and bring a bit of heaven to earth. Compassion's goal is to release children from poverty in Jesus' name by getting sponsors and ministering to the children through a local church. This was a trip to see that in action.

I had read some scripture that morning before going to visit the first project: "If I give all I possess to the poor and give over my body to hardship that I may boast, but do not have love, I gain nothing." 1 Corinthians 13:3 (NIV). What if I give all I have to the poor, if I get people signed up, if I get kids sponsored? You mean, that's not love? How can you do all that and not have it be love?

I realized that I can get so consumed by what I'm supposed to do, that I forget who I'm supposed to be, who God has created me to be, and what he created me for... a relationship with him, to love him, worship him, and enjoy him.

Even ministry can become cold and callused and a form of legalism – an attempt to somehow please or appease God. This can happen when it becomes just a program and you don't see the faces behind it.

Take Haiti, for example. Yes, we are moved by the vastness of the tragedy, and many had their heartstrings tugged enough to give when they suffered the terrible earthquake in January of 2010. I am so thankful for those who were moved to make a difference. But compare that situation to one where you personally knew someone in Haiti and you wanted to know if they were okay. The immense burden and intensity of those emotions pale to the others.

The two scenarios bring me to the point of asking if I really care. Do I have compassion for them, or do I just feel sorry for them and give a small gift to appease my sense of guilt? Did I do it so the next time I hear someone asking me to give I can tell them I already did... basically saying, "Leave me alone; I did my part?"

So there I was, walking into a Compassion project in El Salvador with 171 children in yellow shirts, their "uniform," and each one is waving a brightly colored balloon to welcome us. The smiles melted my heart, and then they sang a few songs. My heart said, "It is working," and I felt good about being a part of this great work. I was so glad my friends were seeing it.

Then the director asked me to step away from the crowds and pray for one student. "Sure," I responded.

The girl I was asked to pray for was maybe 5 or 6 with dark black hair pulled into a pony tail. Her deep brown eyes would melt anyone as they said, "Papa!" I knelt down to get to her level and she reached to grab my hand as the director of the project told me her story.

Her mother died when she was young, and she lived with her Papa whom she adored. But just two weeks ago he was on the bus coming home from work and he fell asleep. Some gang members attacked him, cut him and broke his neck. The director told me, "He died and she is now an orphan. Could you pray for her?"

I've seen it all before? My heart swelled. She isn't an "it!" This isn't about a project, or poverty, or getting sponsors. This isn't about a ministry or someone's vision. This is about a child, a person with a heart and hurts and longings. She is in a situation I can't even imagine, facing what a child should never have to face.

I no longer had to wonder what my heart would feel if this happened to someone I knew... I do know her now. She was holding my hand, looking into my eyes, and hoping my words would somehow reach heaven and comfort her precious soul. Only then could I get a glimpse of what God feels for her.

Never before have I felt so inadequate, so hopeless, and so angry at the effects of poverty. There were no feelings of pride or having done enough. Instead, I felt compelled to do anything I could and give everything I had. Yet I couldn't do anything to take away her pain of losing both parents.

I don't understand what happened next, but as I stumbled over my words in prayer and the tears from the director, the girl and my own joined as one on the ground, and our hearts cried out in desperation together as equals, it was as if I was in the presence of God himself.

This is not about anything but worship. And until we see real people and not projects, real children and not tragedies, we will not see Jesus. Until we see Jesus we'll continue to callously say, "I've seen it all before," and we'll become just another organization with big budgets and grander boasts of what we have done.

Instead, this visit ended with two little arms wrapped around my neck. To be honest, I haven't been so close to Jesus in quite some time.

PRAYER

Break my heart for the needs and hurts of others. Never let me be content and say "I've seen it all before." Help me stay in close relationship to you, Jesus, and love every person around me, as though I were ministering directly to you. There are always more who need to know your love through ours.

Everyone Counts or No One Counts

I'M ON THE ROAD A LOT, so I don't get to take calls from the office as often as I'd like. Instead, I have to rely on my staff to handle many of the things that come in. Our administrative assistant, Jennifer Perry, recently wrote about one such phone call...

"Is Bob there?" The voice was young and female, a little shaky.

It was a Wednesday morning in July, the first day of Lifest, the five-day festival put on by Life Promotions. Bob Lenz, Life Promotions' founder and main speaker, was already down at the festival grounds, along with all my co-workers. I was in the office to field all those frantic "I lost my ticket!" calls before shutting things down and joining them.

"He's not here," I said. "Is there something I can do for you?" The silence lasted so long that I thought maybe she had hung up. Then, very quietly, she said, "Sometimes ... I feel ... like I want to die."

Had she been calling about a lost ticket, I would have known how to help her. But I have no training in crisis management, and there was no one there to guide me. Still, I had one coherent thought, which was that if one of my children had made such a call, I would have wanted the person on the other end of the line to take it very, very seriously.

So I told her that I would try to reach Bob, but in the meantime, I was going to get her some help. I started pawing through the telephone directory by my desk, looking for the number of a local suicide hotline. And then an ominous thought occurred: *Bob speaks to kids all over the country.*

"Where are you calling from?" I asked.

"Pennsylvania."

Oh, God, now what? I did the only thing I could think of: I called 911, told them the situation, and asked if they could get me the emergency number for the town in Pennsylvania where the girl had said she was living. And soon — remarkably soon — I was talking to a young EMT named Corey in Pennsylvania.

By this time, the voice had a name — Ashley — and she had given me her phone number, but she wouldn't tell me her last name or her address. And there was another problem. The phone number she had given me had an Ohio area code.

Corey needed me to check with Ashley that she was really calling from Pennsylvania. (They were both very patient with me as I alternated putting one on hold to talk to the other.) Ashley had lived for a time in Ohio, but was in fact living in Pennsylvania. When I told this to Corey, I thought it would be a simple matter of tracking Ashley through her cell phone. Oddly, it turns out that this is not nearly as easy as they make it seem on TV.

The only way to resolve this was to get Ashley and Corey speaking directly. I asked Ashley if she would promise to call Corey if I promised to keep trying to reach Bob.

And we both kept our word, because Ashley called me the next day, a little bewildered that the police had shown up at her door.

Bob has kept in touch with her, as has another Life Promotions speaker, Tiffany Thompson. The last I heard, she was doing well and had started college.

So what makes a sad teenager in Pennsylvania reach out to a shaggy-haired youth speaker half a continent away?

Bob's message is not unique, but apparently his ability to communicate it is. He is genuine and gentle. He's not slick, or polished, or flashy. He wears jeans and sneakers and untucked shirts. He is completely, utterly unpretentious. He radiates kindness. The person that kids see on their school auditorium stages is exactly the same person that I see whenever he's in the office, which is rarely, because he's usually on a school auditorium stage. He's going to Alaska. In February. On purpose.

Life Promotions is a faith-based organization, but Bob's public-school talks are about things like respect and the value of each person, and no constitutional amendments are harmed in the making of them. Kids respond because the message is delivered with humor and humility, and because it's true.

It's the same basic truth that author Michael Connelly uses as the philosophy of his fictional detective Harry Bosch: Everyone counts, or no one counts.

And since I have you all here, I'm going to do something I rarely do and climb up on a soapbox. (I feel taller already.) School administrators who think that all is well in their institutions because the test scores are decent and the teams are winning need to get their heads out of their nether regions and look around.

Every day, in every school in this country, there are kids who are being subjected to physical, emotional and verbal abuse that wouldn't be tolerated for a minute in the adult workplace. If you were coming to work every day knowing that you would be the target of mocking, bullying and/or physical intimidation, you would make sure that something was done about it. But for some reason, vulnerable, insecure teenagers, many with less-than-ideal home lives, are supposed to just suck it up and deal.

Your halls are full of the walking wounded, and some of them may not survive. Please, please pay attention to them.

Everyone counts, or no one counts.

By: Jennifer Perry

PRAYER

Stir in the hearts of young people to reach out to someone when they're hurting.

ALASKA

"THIS MAY BE THE MOST IMPORTANT THING I've ever done in my life," said Clara. She was our host person who coordinated this trip to Alaska. Eleven days and eighteen presentations: ten school programs, one parent/ teen program, three churches and four outreach rallies. We were in Anchorage, Peters Creek, Chugiak, Wasilla, Palmer, Eagle River and Valdez. Cases of bibles, 150 bible studies, 3,500 follow-up brochures, and a newly designed "Why Suicide?" booklet were given out to parents, churches, youth pastors and counselors to help fight against suicide.

Fellowship was shared during 33 breakings of the bread (meals) where there was salmon and halibut, and sometimes (almost always) pizza.

Prayer times abounded as people cried out to reach their communities. Youth pastors connected with youth they never met. Churches had junior and senior high youth fill their pews. Christians built respect with educators, working alongside them to bring in a top of the line prevention program. Over 130 people came to Christ, and more than 4,000 were touched through the trip.

But how do you measure the hugs, smiles, tears, silence broken, secret pain finally being exposed, single parents encouraged, blended families bonding, traditional families being cheered on, and Christians recommitting to live out their faith? Seeds were sown and hope instilled; forgiveness given and received; people accepted themselves; dreams were dreamed, and healing that came from just the laughter alone, abounded.

Am I exaggerating the effects? Not at all. The word of God says that His word will not come back void... "so is my word that goes out from my mouth: It will not return to me empty, but will accomplish what I desire and achieve the purpose for which I sent it." – Isaiah 55:11 (NIV)

Ephesians 3:20 is proven true once again when He shows that He does infinitely and abundantly more than we could hope or ask. When Jesus is involved, then the scripture in John 21:25 applies when it says that all the books in the world cannot contain what He has done. This is how I feel about our trip to Alaska.

The biggest and most fulfilling part was the relationships that were built with God and one another. We had countless principals, counselors, parents and health professionals who said, "Next time you come I can get you into such and such school..." There's a pastor in Fairbanks who wanted me to speak during our time there, although we couldn't make it, yet he said he'd bring us back. Sheri Beck, our contact who brought us into Valdez, wants to help organize outreach programs to all the surrounding communities.

And oh, yeah... Clara, the person who set all of this up in the first place, raised the money and built the teams. Clara, through God you have altered eternity.

And I want you to know that all the work, effort, tears and struggles are worth it... for the 16 year old dressed in black who shared how he's been bullied for being in a special speech class and made fun of for being slower in math and has been physically abused by his father. But instead of letting his pain turn into vengeance and the vengeance turning him into another school shooter, he came and shared his story, breaking down in tears as he threw his arms around me and gave me a huge hug. Then he came to the evening rally with his mom who was recently divorced because of the abuse. They got there 35 minutes early and sat together in the second row of pews and drank in more messages of hope.

It's worth it... for the native Alaskan who was raised in Nome by his alcoholic parents and was taken away from them; who now lives in a foster home in Anchorage and saw us at his high school. He came to the evening outreach and received Christ.

It's worth it... for the students at Gurney, where close to 60% have a parent in the military and 40% of the school population has a parent deployed in the Middle East. We got to honor them as we showed and taught about respect.

It's worth it... for Daryl, a boy at a rally whose mom just died of cancer, whose dad was in prison, and who is now living with a church family. He was at our evening rally where by "chance/God's plan" he was randomly picked by AJ the Animated Illusionist to be on stage as part of his presentation. I was backstage at the time and didn't know it, but when I gave my talk I randomly picked the same boy to receive a free shirt as part of my demonstration that grace is a free gift. Then, when we had the drawing after the program, his name was picked to win a free CD. At this time we did not know his story, but God did. He used every circumstance to penetrate deep into Daryl's heart.

Daryl raised his hand, one of only five that received Christ that night. Afterwards, the pastor told us his story, and we marveled once again at God's amazing and beautiful plan.

"A cheerful heart is good medicine, but a crushed spirit dries up the bones." – *Proverbs 17:22 (NIV)*

UPDATE: If you combine all the time our team has spent in Alaska over the past 6 years, it adds up to about 2/3 of a year. Clara, who is half Alaskan native, has a powerful testimony and a desire to reach back to her people. She has since brought our team back to do even more programs and reach more youth. Sheri has also worked with us on other trips. Her son, Cole, has since interned with Life Promotions and even came on board to work for a summer and toured with me and the Newsboys to 60 cities across the US. The impact of this trip is reaching far beyond Alaska.

PRAYER

"Let me never grow weary in telling about you, for only you can bring this kind of hope."

I Never Wanted to Be "*That Guy*"...

ALL I EVER WANTED TO DO with my life was to have an impact on youth; to help them deal with the daily issues they're facing and show them where real life and real hope comes from. There are two things I never wanted to be...

#1 – a "*motivational speaker.*" You know, the one who's perceived as the guy who lives in the back of his van down by the river, as was made popular by Chris Farley on Saturday Night Live. He overzealously tried to get kids to just forget their problems and straighten up by having "positive thinking." I never wanted to be that guy.

#2 – I never wanted to be an "*evangelist*" – or at least perceived as one. This time it was because of the very real and negative images of some television evangelists. I heard that, instead of having an evangelist as a neighbor, most people would rather live next door to a drug lord, a prostitute ring or a used car salesman (sorry if you sell cars

– I didn't write the survey)! Still, it's so sad and backwards because an evangelist is supposed to be a bringer of good news.

For a guy who never wanted to be either of those things, I haven't done very well, because now I'm both.

I'm officially *"that guy."*

I spend time in the public schools as a motivational speaker, telling teens about their inherent value, how they should stand up for others who are being put down and bullied, and encouraging them to press on in an ever-evolving culture and world. Then in the evening we partner with the faith community and invite kids to a rally where I can share the Good News of Jesus. My hope and prayer is to tear down the negative stereotypes and leave a better image and taste of both roles as we seek to talk about real life and real faith, for this life and the next. More importantly, I want to leave a better image and taste of Jesus. I guess that's what an evangelist really is.

A recent trip to Minnesota affirmed to me the sometimes neglected aspect of being and becoming a biblical evangelist. It's an important part of my role that I forget to ask prayer for. The bible says in Ephesians 4:11-12 "So Christ himself gave the apostles, the prophets, the evangelists, the pastors and teachers, to equip his people for works of service, so that the body of Christ may be built up." (*NIV*) My role as an evangelist is not just to evangelize non-churched youth, but to train, equip and encourage people to win their friends for Christ. This is especially important in light of the reality that the vast majority of people never allow God to use them to lead another person to Christ.

My team and I will never stop evangelizing youth, but we want to be more intentional of our mission to reach American youth by calling other Christians to become "missional" in all they do, with all that they have, and in their relationships. That's when we can really multiply evangelism efforts and see even more people come to Christ. It's not just the pastor's job, or the youth leader's job, or the evangelist's job. Each person has a responsibility to share the love and hope they've found in Christ.

My trip to Minnesota brought us to North Central University to speak at a chapel for all the students majoring in Youth Studies. These young people were pursuing going into youth ministry, and their education encouraged and trained them to have a heart for evangelism. Just think of the impact all these people can have.

I also got to team up with Faith Inkubators out of Stillwater, MN. I was in front of church leaders from

Australia who were being trained for 3 weeks on reaching and keeping the next generation for Christ. The U.S. currently has about 43% of the people attending church of some kind,[1] but in Australia it's only 8%,[2] so I got to share and train on the importance of using youth in evangelism. It was a fantastic time of connecting with other brothers and sisters in another nation with the same passion for reaching youth.

During the next two days I got to do chapel services at Northwestern College for 1,200 students. This college was started by one of the greatest evangelists that has ever lived – Billy Graham. I saw in that audience hope for our nation, an excitement for the church and a passion for the lost. We ended our time there by having an evening outreach with over 30 youth groups coming together to be encouraged as they start up the new school year, training them to be witnesses in their schools.

As I was speaking on the need to love in Jesus' name and to stick to the core of the gospel, I also gave an opportunity for people to respond and receive Christ. Even though it was an event for churched youth, thirty of them came to Jesus! I then saw 300 of the 500 students stand and make a commitment to win their schools for Christ. I think we will hear many stories from the road when we get to heaven of all the impact those kids will have in that area.

I will no longer apologize for being *"that guy."* Instead, I want to convince others to be that guy or that girl, and to be the best motivational speakers and best evangelists they can be in all aspects of their lives.

I guess I do want to be "that guy" after all... that guy who *"brings the good news of salvation"* (Isaiah 52:7). We should all desire to be "that guy" to those around us.

PRAYER

God, thank you for who you have made me as an individual, and help me to walk in my calling and do what you've called me to do. Thank you that you were "that guy," and may I follow in your footsteps to bring the Good News to the world.

It's Urgent

ur·gent (ûr-jent) *adj.*

1. Something that requires immediate action or attention

2. Of pressing importance

3. Too pressing to permit a longer delay

SOMETIMES I FORGET THE URGENCY. Why? Sometimes I feel like I can take any story from the 1980's, 90's or last few years, and they all sound the same. Only the name, place and date would change.

There are so many tragic stories of youth without hope, beaten down by broken families, abandonment, abuse, and addictions from their own choices and those of others. We may be talking about eating disorders, cutting, bullying, school shootings, teen pregnancies, the dropout rate, gangs, blurred lines of sexuality or violence, not to mention the normal self-image issues of adolescence.

Then throw on top of that the onslaught of moral

decay from the media and entertainment world, the internet, and the reality of war and the fear of terrorism.

Many of the needs seem the same, but the answer also remains the same: hope. Teens need hope to deal with the here and now for a better tomorrow. But my deepest desire is for them to receive a hope in Christ for real life. If that reality doesn't cause a sense of urgency, then add this to it:

66% of youth who come to that hope in a personal faith in Christ, do so before the age of 18.[1]

It's urgent! We've proclaimed these truths and lived in that state of urgency since the ministry began nearly 30 years ago. It's easy to grow weary and tired, or become complacent and say, "What can I do?"

Do what God assigned you to do – no more and no less.

Many stories through the years can sound the same, but we can't let them blend together. They're still individuals – unique, valuable, and with their own personal story. And as much as we will try to continue to reach the masses with the gospel of Jesus, please know it's all for just one. It's worth all the time, energy, money and sacrifice. They are not in vain. The stakes are too high.

A parent called to have me come and speak at the school in her community. She was shaken to her core and wanted me to come as soon as possible. She told how that same day a girl had walked home after classes. It was her 18th birthday, and she got all dressed up for the occasion. She was beautiful and now had a dress to match. If only her dad could see her, or the beautiful artwork she created: pictures drawn, sculptures carved, poems written.

But her dad wasn't there to see them or her, for he had been gone for years. Somehow with him, so went her hope and worth. Replacing it in her heart were pain, anger and questions.

Much of her art reflected her struggle within. Somehow all the art and carvings weren't therapeutic enough, though, because that day she began carving on herself to numb the pain. The red blood highlighted her white dress. It was sprinkled throughout the house as if she danced her last dance. The distraught parent on the phone wept as she told me, "She said a final good bye with the bang of a gun."

She was gone at 18... forever.

It's just one story of tragedy, but it's about someone's baby girl, and it cries out, "It's urgent!" Every life matters.

PRAYER

There are days I feel helpless to address all the pain and struggles that teens face. Thank you, God, that it's not by my power, but Yours. Still, please give me an urgency to make every breath count and to touch every life I can.

Fruit. And the Fruit that Remains.

A GRANDMA CAME UP TO ME after my talk, with tears running down her face. "Thank you! Thank you! Thank you!" she said. "My eight year old grandson sat on my lap and could not take his eyes off you during your whole talk. He held on to every word you spoke. When you gave the invitation to receive Christ, his hand was the first one that went up!"

She continued, "I've been praying for him to know the love of Jesus. When you asked people to come and get a Bible and follow up material, he didn't even ask me. He jumped up out of my arms and ran to the prayer tent." His faith life is just beginning.

I met this woman and her grandson at a Christian music festival called AtlantaFest, where I gave the keynote address before Skillet played. School was out for the summer, but one thing that remains the same throughout every season is evangelism. For the summer, the venues just look a little different. I may be at festivals instead of schools and rallies, but whenever God allows me to be in front of an audience, my heart longs to bring people into a relationship with Jesus.

When people hear about a young boy like that eight year old, they often ask, "Do you think it's real? Do you think it lasts? Do you think they become disciples? Or is it just emotion?" Perhaps that can be best answered with another story from someone I met right after I met that grandma.

My wife, Carol, introduced me to another woman and said, "You have to hear her story, Bob."

"My name is Jo," she said. "I'm from Oshkosh, Wisconsin." I was surprised to see someone from Oshkosh all the way in Georgia. She went on to tell me, "A friend brought me to your Christian festival, Lifest, 11 years ago. I did not know Jesus when I came, but I met Him there and He changed my life. I want to thank you and your team for putting on Lifest, and for you speaking at it. I am a Christian today because of it."

My heart swelled with joy, and my eyes welled with tears as she continued, "The fall after I went to Lifest I went away to college at UW Madison. There, I got involved with Campus Crusade for Christ. I think my parents thought I was crazy or in a cult, because for spring break I went down to an outreach in inner city Chicago instead of a drunken beach in Florida." We laughed together.

"It took me five years to finally get my parents to come to Lifest," she said. "But now, they both love it and get their tickets a year in advance. Since then, they have both put their trust in Christ. I now live down here in Atlanta for my job, but I come back every year for Lifest, and this year my dad is volunteering on the stage crew. I want you to know that what you do matters."

This never gets old, hearing stories of changed lives. I asked Jo why she was at AtlantaFest. She told me she was volunteering for Compassion International. "My parents and I now sponsor children because we want to make a difference in this world," she explained.

Eleven years later she is still serving God, all because of the foolishness of sharing the gospel at Lifest. I've since been able to meet her family at Lifest and pray with them. I even brought Jo up on stage to share her story of how God has been faithful.

Fruit remains. She was 17 years old when she first came and heard about Jesus. Now look what she is doing.

This begs me to ask you to pray for that 8 year old boy. Just imagine where he will be and who he will be impacting eleven years from now.

PRAYER

Thank you for your faithfulness and relentless pursuit of your children. I pray for the fruit to remain in all those who come to you, and for it to be seen by this world to give you glory.

Hope After the Storm

I REMEMBER IT LIKE IT WAS YESTERDAY, even though it's been years. It was devastating. It was like when suicide strikes a family; tragedy did not discriminate between rich and poor, good and bad, or Christian and non-Christian. Nothing I saw on TV captured how bad it was.

Hurricane Katrina.

We sent a mission team of young people to the area a couple months afterward. Their main job was gutting people's homes and throwing away *every* possession they had. Once all that was on the curb, they ripped out all the drywall. Mold was everywhere.

The worst part of every house was the refrigerator. They were full of floodwater mixed with rancid rotting food that sat entombed for almost two months in the hot and humid Louisiana climate. The smell was overwhelming and instantly activated every gag reflex.

This area was considered the "salvageable" part of

town. It was the community of Chalmette, which sits east of downtown New Orleans. The entire city is expected to be bulldozed to the ground. Everything is lost.

Now two months later, it was my turn. As we drove during the first week of December to the school where I was supposed to speak, my heart sank at the desolation. Street after street. House after house. Abandoned. A pickup truck in a tree. A house in the middle of the road where it had landed after coming off its foundation. A levy wall broken.

The despair was thick. It was like a ghost town. I felt overwhelmed, like a grain of sand in an ocean of anguish and loss.

The school district used to have 14 schools and all were closed after Katrina. They were able to recently reopen one that combined all the grades together. Where normally more than 14,000 students would gather for classes, only 200 were able to make it back.

The principal of the school I visited that day lost his house and both cars. I talked to 5 teachers that lost everything, including their jobs. Four months later, they now live 60 miles away and drive in every day so they can be there for the kids. No jobs. No home. Nothing. To even remotely grasp the loss of this community, it's as simple as doing an internet search to read newspaper headlines, see the television reports, and view photos from the weeks following Katrina.

Still, I spoke. It's what I've been called to do. If I can convince just one more student to not give into despair, then I will have made a difference. When I was done speaking, the principal walked up to me in front of all the students and said, "We have a new tradition since Katrina: We hug our friends when we leave them." This 60 year old man who has weathered many storms in his long life had never seen the likes of Katrina. He started crying and gave me a huge hug in front of his entire student body.

May these people, our nation and this world not miss the good that can come from a tragedy – people pulling together, people living on less, people seeing value not in things, but in life, faith, and people working together to let others know that hope can be found in what seems the most hopeless of situations, and that love conquers all.

We almost always charge schools for our programs to help cover expenses, but in certain cases we waive our fees and do them anyway. This is why.

PRAYER

Father, comfort those who are experiencing loss today. Help me be your hands and feet to be part of bringing that comfort.

From Sea to Shining Sea

IT WAS APRIL 9, 2011 and I arrived at the venue in Maryland just minutes before I was to go on stage to speak. I was still in the same clothes I had worn at the rally the night before in British Columbia Canada. John, my road manager, told me not to worry. "They don't know what you wore yesterday," he said. "And besides, the audience is far enough away that they can't smell you."

I spent the previous four days in British Columbia doing eight school assembly programs and four rallies, seeing hundreds come to Christ. From Canada, we drove through the night to get to the Seattle airport to catch a 6am flight to Washington, DC because I needed to meet up with a tour that started the next day in Maryland. Someone picked me up in DC and drove another two hours to connect me with the tour which included Kutless, Newsboys, Carlos Whittaker and Disciple.

God has blessed me to be able to speak in so

many audiences and venues, including schools, churches, festivals, arenas, cars and planes.

That night I was in Williamsport, MD, with people being touched by the love of God. As soon as I was done speaking, I jumped in a truck with Dave King, a friend who puts on a youth festival called iMatter. We drove through the night for 6½ hours to his hometown in upstate New York. After spending a couple hours sleeping on a couch, I preached for his church's Sunday morning service – a message calling the church back to evangelism. Afterwards, I had lunch with the pastors and leaders of the church. From that meeting we were able to set up schools and rallies in their community for the fall in a place called Mexico, NY. After lunch, we drove another two hours to catch back up with the tour for another show in Binghamton, NY.

After speaking that night, I got to sleep on the bus for the first time as we drove to the next city. I imagine it's like sleeping in a coffin. Not that I would know. But it's hard when the sleeping unit on the bus is only 6' long and I'm 6'4". Do the math. We made it to the next city to do it all over again.

Now, nearly two months later, I woke up in Sacramento, CA. I think. It has been a whirlwind. We still have 8 cities left on the tour. We've been in 17 cities already, and in front of more than 30,000 people, preaching every night to groups as large as 4,000, averaging 1,600 a night.

I miss my bed. I miss my wife. I miss my family. Whoever said traveling was glamorous?

Please don't hear me complaining. Okay, I am complaining. But this is also so much fun. I know I'm doing exactly what I feel God has called me to do and made me to be. It's like a dream come true: Instilling hope and sharing the gospel with people, and calling people to live out God's love in a tangible way.

There were stories of pain and opportunities to offer comfort. I heard stories of loss and new beginnings. Stories of guilt and of forgiveness being received. Stories of people once battling addiction, now experiencing freedom.

I've been gone 62 out of the last 74 days. There was an outpouring and overflowing of God's love and God's call, feeling God's word and spirit sustained. I just spoke at a concert in Kentucky where we saw 120 people respond to the gospel, with 62 of those being for the first time.

A couple weeks ago in Phoenix, a 15 year old girl came up to me. All she said was, "Can I have a hug?" It was like hugging one of my own daughters. I felt like my hug was saying, "It's okay. I don't know what's going on right now, but God does. He understands. You are loved."

If you're a parent, you know what I'm talking about. She looked up at me with a tear in her eye and said, "Thank you. You really touched my life." She walked away. I figured she was probably going to get a Newsboys autograph. She didn't want mine.

But then a guy walked up to me and said, "I'm her adopted dad. Her biological family is a total mess and her dad's in prison. Her sister who is a year older than her is institutionalized with an addiction and just attempted suicide."

I was stunned, wishing I would have hugged her just a moment longer or said something.

"Jesus just reached my daughter through your words," he said. "I've not been able to break the shell she's put up around her heart, but somehow God did it by His spirit tonight." He looked at me more intensely and said, "You don't know what this means to me." He now had a tear in his eye.

All I could think was, "I have to get back on that bus. I have to go to another city. I have to do this again... from sea to shining sea. Why? Because Christ isn't just the hope of that teenage girl; He truly is the hope for the world."

PRAYER

Whose eyes have I looked into and just allowed them to pass by without saying, "I care," or "God loves you?" Help me to see past the outward smile into their soul, to touch their soul with your love. May your passion spur me on, no matter how difficult it seems at times.

An Unwilling Servant

I WALKED INTO A RESTROOM at a gas station that happened to have a baby changing station. Above it hung a sign with bold letters: "Not for cleaning fish." I laughed so hard. I was in a little town in northern Wisconsin called Rhinelander, home of the "Hodags." The hodag is a fictional dinosaur-like creature found in the folklore of 19th-century lumberjacks, and it lives on as this town's school mascot. That's the kind of unique place the Rhinelander area is. It's "up north" for those who live further south - dotted with lakes, surrounded by forests, known for hunting, fishing, and snowmobiling.

The last time I was in Rhinelander, more than 350 youth came out to our rally, so this time we had high expectations. We were already planning on being in the area for a few days, so it made sense to schedule a Saturday night youth event in hopes of a nice kick-off to the school programs that would begin on Monday morning.

Instead of 350, only 70 people came that Saturday night. Disappointment hit my heart, and I felt bad for the sponsors. But then I remembered a time in my life years ago when God used an even smaller crowd to get my attention...

I received a call from a pastor asking me to speak to 300 youth, and I was so excited. I had never spoken to that many people. The promise of an offering was my only financial guarantee, and I had to drive five hours just to get there. But I didn't care – I knew this was my calling in life. All the way there I kept thinking, "I'm going to speak to 300 kids!" I got there and sure enough, there were 300 chairs ... but only 18 people.

I wasn't just disappointed. I was mad! But God wouldn't let me stay trapped in that anger.

A few minutes before my time to speak, the pastor asked me to pray with him and a few adult leaders in his office. He closed his eyes and began, "Lord, if it's all for one, it's worth it all." I was so angry that I couldn't even close my eyes. I peered around the room looking for anything on the walls to distract me so I wouldn't hit this pastor. He hadn't driven five hours. He was getting paid. And me? I was going to get an offering from 18 high school kids. My attitude stunk.

As I looked around the room my eyes came upon a poster of Jesus and his disciples tacked to the wall with a caption that read, "His youth group changed the world."

Ouch.

My heart melted and I was hit with the conviction of God's love. I might have driven five hours, but Jesus came all the way from heaven. I had eighteen. He had only twelve. I was just Bob, and He was God. For three years, Jesus invested in those twelve. All I was asked to do was give a talk for an hour. I promised on that day, 24 years ago, that I would always give my all to reach youth, no matter what, because they matter.

So, this time when I was in Rhinelander, I was reminded of that night so many years before, but with a much better attitude. Our team was determined to give those 70 youth our best. The band rocked out as though they had thousands in the audience. Then I came up and shared the good news of Jesus.

God moved and brought salvation to seven youth that night. Seven! Yes, 10% of the audience received Christ. And dozens more made a commitment to live out their faith and share it with their friends.

There was so much excitement among the youth to bring their friends to an upcoming "See You at the Pole" rally and introduce them to Jesus. They left the church that night inspired and challenged to change their world. I was humbled once again, and I thought ...

"Okay God, I remember. It's worth it. Really, it is worth it all just for one of those precious kids."

PRAYER

Help me remember, Father, that it's not about the size of the crowd, but the size of our God, and that every person matters. Bring to my mind someone who you want me to reach out to, invest in or mentor.

New From the Inside Out

WE HAD SIX SCHOOL ASSEMBLY PROGRAMS and a rally scheduled. Things were going really well during the first few programs. The students were enjoying the band during the earlier programs, laughing hard at the jokes, and sometimes even crying during the serious moments of my talk that shared about the consequences of bad choices. It's just such an awesome feeling when the message of truth penetrates hearts and people change.

From there we went to a school that was quite large. The gym couldn't accommodate all the students at once, so they gave us their freshman class first. In walked 600 squirrelly 14 and 15-year-olds

Pockets of kids in the crowd seemed almost completely uninterested - and that attitude can spread quickly in a high school gym. I battled for their attention and worked hard to reel them back in over and over again. The band had been seeing great responses from students all week long. But at this school, a few students decided to make it tough for them. The kids turned to one of their friends and urged him to start head banging. And it wasn't hard to see why they chose this guy.

Tyler looked exactly like the kind of kid who many people think would start trouble. He wore black clothing from head to toe. His long, dyed-black hair covered half his face and hung well below his shoulders. He began head banging to the music, bouncing his head back and forth. Hair was flying everywhere, and kids started laughing.

Eventually Tyler and a couple of his pals were kicked out of the auditorium and put in a room where they were forced to sit and listen to my talk.

It was definitely one of the hardest school programs I had been through in years. Our team felt like the day had gone badly, but teachers told us they couldn't believe how well the students listened compared to the way they treated previous speakers. They told us ours was one of the best assemblies they had ever had. We even got a recommendation from the Vice Principal.

As we prepared for the rally that Wednesday night we talked about our rough day, and we honestly wondered if anyone would come back for more. The auditorium looked almost empty up until just before we were scheduled to start, seeming to confirm our fears. But in the last ten minutes, more than 500 youth poured in and we ended up with more than 600 in attendance. The bleachers were packed, except for an area off to the side where a guy was sitting all by himself. I later found out that people actually got up and moved when this person sat down.

It was Tyler.

Apparently the same friends who were all around that afternoon weren't there for him that night. The guy in black, the joker, the kid who was kicked out of the assembly, sat there alone and listened, longing to hear something, anything, that would bring him purpose and meaning. How could he know that I would speak about how it doesn't matter if you are the football captain, a cheerleader, or a student who wears black and is into the Goth scene?

God knew. And He moved in Tyler's heart that night.

I can't write fast enough right now because I suspect you know where this is leading. When I asked the audience if they wanted to trust Jesus with their lives, more than 160 hands went up - and Tyler's was among them. And it gets better - out of that 160, Tyler was one of the

80 people who indicated on follow-up cards that this was their first time responding to the Gospel – new converts for Christ.

Every one of those hands is cause for celebration, but Tyler holds a special place in my heart, because of that first impression he made on me. He was a kink in my day, a distraction, a troublemaker who thoroughly looked the part. And now, by God's grace, I see him in a new light. He's a real person with real hurts, real wounds, and real needs. And, praise God, he's found real Hope.

He also found a lot of love that night. Someone traveling with the band gave him a free copy of their CD. The follow-up team handed him a free bible. Then I spoke with Tyler and he told me he wanted to be baptized. Whoa! I introduced him to a local pastor and gave him one of our Life Survival Guide bible studies to help him grow in his faith. We prayed together, after which the youth pastor looked at him and said, "If you don't have a church, you're sure welcome at our youth group."

What a sweet sound that must have been to Tyler's ears. After being shunned only an hour earlier and left to sit alone, now he was being warmly invited to connect with others who wanted to spend time with him. That's the beauty of the Body of Christ.

Tyler's story is a wake-up call to all of us who want to reach youth for Jesus! Let's stop judging based on what we see on the surface, by appearance and even behavior. On the inside Tyler was a young man longing for a savior, longing to be healed and made new.

PRAYER

Father, help me view people the way you do - from the inside out. Convict me of the times when I've judged someone, or viewed them as a problem to be fixed instead of a person to be loved.

You Can Almost Hear the Angels

THREE DAYS OF SCHOOLS & rallies were scheduled. In total, there were six schools and 5,000 students, plus three rallies averaging 350 in attendance each night, and more than 75 responding to the gospel for the 1st time at each rally. That's 225 receiving the love of Jesus and trusting the gospel!

You can almost hear the angels rejoicing.

Almost. I have a hard time going on with this story because I know how much you probably love youth and hope for this ministry to continue to have results like this. I have a confession: The story above never happened. If you're not too mad at me, will you please read on and see what really did happen?

See, I was booked to speak at a weekend conference with Youth Encounter in Billings, Montana. A friend of the ministry, who also lived in Montana, contacted us to see if we could come to his community to do school programs and outreaches around that same time. His son served with Life Promotions as an intern and he believes wholeheartedly in our ministry. He was also a school teacher for more than 30 years and served as a student council advisor, so he is well-respected and a well-connected person within the community. We set aside three days preceding the conference to speak at six different schools. He wanted more and was determined to make it happen.

He was so excited and began meeting with school administrators to plan. One principal met him with open arms and shared about the great needs of the kids and how the students needed to hear a quality program on prevention. As they continued speaking, however, the plan slowly seemed to slip out of reach. The principal simply stated, "If we had $500 - $1000 to spend, we would choose to get new computers for the students instead. School funding has been cut once again and our computer lab hasn't been updated in 13 years."

Disappointed, our friend went on to the next school and was met with a similar story, only this principal said, "If we had the money we would buy books." They didn't even have enough books for all the students. At each school the response was the same.

This economic hard time has hit us all and even affected budgets at schools. The stress of the economy has also affected families, and youth are dealing with more issues on account of it than ever. It's a dilemma, because as the economy declines, the opportunities to address the increasing needs that result from it go up.

If we could, we would just do the programs for free. But the costs of flights and travel, sound equipment, meals, a quality opening act, lodging, a road manager, bibles, follow up materials and other expenses make it impossible to do it for nothing. I truly wish we could.

With much regret, the three days of schools and rallies had to be cancelled. As I think of it, a knot grabs my stomach and won't let go. I still spoke at the weekend conference, and after talking with our ministry friend, we were able to donate one program at a school in his hometown: Lewis & Clark Middle School in Billings, Montana.

There were 650 students. They laughed so hard at my embarrassing moments, and their eyes filled with tears when I spoke about the hard issues many of them face. The assembly program ended with a standing ovation. The principal later said that it was the best program he'd seen in 27 years of teaching. "We have to get you and this message into every school," he told me. "We're ready and eager to come," I thought. "But how?"

We were able to arrange for student council leaders to attend from other schools to see the program as well. I'm hoping that they can catch the vision and get others to raise the money so we can come back and recapture those opportunities that were lost.

I weep as I write this. Five schools cancelled. Three rallies never happened. Hundreds of youth didn't have a chance to hear the gospel and come to Christ. I know from theology that God is bigger than all of this, but I also know that we have a responsibility to do our part. Youth need prevention programs in their schools and need Jesus more than ever.

We need people to pray. We need people to come together and bring us in to different schools. We need people to step up in their community so messages of hope can fill the hallways of our junior and senior high schools and the hearts of students. We need people to provide for scholarships that offer these programs in communities that can't afford to bring us in. I know things are tight, but we can't stop now.

I don't know about you, but I don't want to *almost* hear the angels. They are waiting with anticipation for a reason to rejoice, and I want to hear them loud and clear. Let's never stop sharing the love of God.

PRAYER

God, stir the hearts of those you've called to become a part of bringing the gospel to youth across this nation and the world.

HOPE

I USUALLY SHARE MY OWN STORIES, but I feel compelled to include this one that was written by my assistant, Tammy...

This wasn't a typical rally. More than 1,200 people showed up to fill an auditorium with 800 seats. So we had to ask people who had seen Bob and AJ the Animated Illusionist before to be willing to give up their spots. Still not enough room. Then we asked parents to give up their seats so more kids could hear the message.

The response to having Bob and AJ in the schools was so positive that it seemed the entire community came out. The reality is that the programs in this community had received a lot of publicity, but not for positive reasons. You see, the programs were organized in response to a rash of recent tragedies. Four students had taken their own lives in the past six months. The most recent was less than a month ago – a 15 year old sophomore boy.

After a 20 minute delay to get everyone seated, the program began. The night hadn't gone quite as I had planned. I had intended to assist AJ with one of his illusions by being the disappearing girl... but apparently disappearing people need to be really flexible. So the disappearing act didn't take place, but I did get to sit backstage and wait for the cue to bring out AJ's beloved performing dog, Bear, for his part of the opening show. Though I couldn't see the audience from behind the stage curtain, I could tell that hearts were softening and laughter was bringing healing.

AJ finished and Bob Lenz took the stage to speak. I remained backstage for a while, helping AJ pack up some things. Then I decided to go out to the commons area to see if I could help there, but the youth leaders had everything under control. I wanted to take some photos of Bob on stage as he spoke, but I knew I couldn't go inside the auditorium that was already at full capacity. Someone suggested I go to the sound booth to get some photos from there. When I climbed the stairs and turned the corner, I quickly realized it was too dark to get any good shots. So, I decided to just hang out until the program ended.

I could see down on the crowd from there. Every seat was filled. I tried to see if there was anyone I recognized, but it was difficult from the back. I can't explain why, maybe it was the pattern of her black and white hounds-tooth coat that stood out to me, but I particularly noticed a woman who sat against the wall, with a man seated next to her. Maybe it was because the room was mostly filled with students that these adults stood out to me. They were listening intently and I felt prompted to say a little prayer for them.

Bob continued sharing about the love of Christ. Then, that most important moment came when heads are bowed, eyes are closed and the ear of God is bent a little closer to the earth, anticipating a whisper from the heart that says, "Yes, I believe." He was not disappointed. As Bob invited people to respond to the gospel and trust in God's love, literally hundreds of hands went up in the air: young and old, boy and girl, including the man and woman I had noticed earlier. Tears came to my eyes as I looked down on a sea of people, who only moments ago I couldn't find anything in common with, but now I could call them my brothers and sisters. So many had come and found a lasting hope.

Things wrapped up on stage and people began piling out after the program to get their free pizza. Those who responded to the message were given a free workbook, along with Bob's book *Grace,* as a result of the generosity of many people from a local church. I wanted to cut through the flow of traffic to go backstage and help pack up, but getting through was going to be difficult. So, I paused on the edge of the crowd, waiting for an opportunity.

Suddenly I heard my name, "Tammy, how are you?" I gazed into the eyes of a woman who was about my age. She looked vaguely familiar, and I'm sure she saw the wheels turning in my head as I thought, "Where do I know you from?" She could tell the answer wasn't coming quickly and generously offered the information. "It's Rita, remember?" she said. "I graduated a year ahead of you. I recognized you when you brought the little dog out on stage."

Suddenly, it came to me. Her eyes hadn't changed since the last time I saw her 25 years ago. But there was something in them that made me wonder what life had brought her in those years. We were merely acquaintances back in high school, having some mutual friends and extracurricular activities, but never really engaging in conversations or spending much time together.

"Yes! I remember you," I said. Not really knowing what to say, I stated the usual, "How have you been?" She seemed to offer the usual response, "I'm okay."

There was that moment of awkwardness that always comes when two people who haven't seen each other in years come face to face again, having lost any connection they might have once had. A sea of people pressed against us, willing us to move downstream, but we temporarily fought against the tide to continue exchanging pleasantries.

"Did you enjoy the program?" I asked. "Oh yes, it was wonderful," she said. "I came to the parent program last week too. It was so good." "That's great," I responded.

What she said next stunned me. The words didn't match her glimmering eyes and I found myself wondering if I heard her right among the excited chatter of passers by.

"We came because of my son, Lucas. He was the last one to commit suicide." My heart sank, instantly turning from a feeling of joy over reconnecting with an old acquaintance, to horror at what I just heard.

Tears welled in my eyes and the only words I could find were, "Oh, I'm so sorry." I reached out to hug her and we embraced. It was one of those real hugs where you linger a little longer than usual. "I'm so sorry," I said again. What could I say? It had been less than a month since her son had taken his own life.

"Thanks for tonight," she said. "It's good to know there are so many people who care and want to help."

I wanted to pull her aside and talk, but the crowd pushed stronger and she gestured that she was ready to give in to the throng of people streaming out of the auditorium. "It was good to see you," she said. "You too," I replied. "Take care..." And she slipped back into the crowd.

I stepped back for a moment, holding back the tears. What just happened? The conversation maybe lasted a minute, but it left me heartbroken. Questions flooded my mind. Would I see her again? Would she be okay? What could possibly take away the pain she was experiencing? What could possibly restore her hope?

The answers to my haunting questions came as I glanced back for one last look to see her walk away... with her black and white hounds-tooth coat draped softly over her shoulders.

There was hope. The giver of hope had taken up residence in her soul, and in the hearts of countless others that night. I felt a rush of emotion and turned to face the oncoming crowd once again; my heart strangely at peace.

By: Tammy Borden

PRAYER

God, comfort the broken-hearted in the way only You can.

Fishing for Men

CITY FOLKS WOULD SAY I was in the middle of nowhere. I was in Barriere, British Columbia Canada, which is six hours northeast of Seattle, WA. I preached at Christian Life Assembly, an awesome body of believers. Many brought friends and family and we had over 90 people in their Sunday service. The week before with summer absences they had 30. It was so fun to see them adding more chairs.

But the most awesome thing was seeing 10 people trust Christ for salvation. After the church service, Roger, a new friend, offered to bring me out fishing that afternoon. How could I refuse fishing in Canada? We drove 10 miles from the middle of nowhere out of town. Then we drove 25 miles up a mountain on a gravel road. They called it a road; I called it a trail. I hit my head on the roof of the truck three times with the excessive bouncing, waking me up from my afternoon nap after preaching.

We finally got to the lake. Well, kind of. I couldn't

even see the lake until Roger led me to the edge of the mountain we'd just climbed to look down a massive hill. From there all I could see was amazing beauty and I stood in awe of God's wild creation. Then I saw the lake below. The name of the lake was No Man's Lake. It was not even on the map we had.

As I peered down I asked where the boat landing was. Roger chuckled. There wasn't one. I looked back at the 14 foot aluminum boat on top of his 350 Diesel Ford truck, along with the nine horse Mercury motor, the poles, the paddles and all the gear. I looked back down the hill, afraid to ask the obvious, "How are we going to get there with no boat landing?" Roger smiled and said, "We're going to carry it down that path."

In my mind, all I could scream was, "Are you kidding me!?!" But Roger was about 10 years older than me, so my pride kept me from complaining too much. Besides, he said there were rainbow trout in this lake.

So, there I was, huffing and puffing as we carried the boat and all the gear... and this was going down the hill. All my mind could think was "How are we ever going to get it back up there?"

We finally got on the lake. We didn't see one car all the way in. There wasn't one building on the whole lake.

And we didn't see one other boat. We had no fancy fish finder, depth finder or underwater camera. No big modern technology. Just a simple spinning rod, reel, and a little Mepps spinner.

Within five minutes we had three trout. Roger laughed and said, "This isn't fishing. This is catching."

We ended up with 12, two over our limit. So we threw two back. What an unforgettable fishing trip. As the joy of catching such beauties swelled inside me, I had forgotten about all the hard work. This is why we came: to catch fish. Sure, I was huffing, okay, almost dying on the way back up the hill! But the satisfaction of the catch made it worth it all.

We are called to go fishing: Evangelism. We're also called to go where the people are because we don't want to go to a lake where there aren't any fish! At Life Promotions, we could just do conferences, but we want to go where the kids are, so we present programs in the schools, followed by evangelistic rallies at night.

It's hard. It's a lot of work. It's heartbreaking. Hearing stories of kids day after day, sharing about their pain and brokenness, makes our hearts heavy, almost to the point of depression.

There are days when we have to set up a sound system three different times. You get tired and lonely, being away from family and realizing your wife is a single mom for half the year.

It costs a lot, paying for entertainment and pizza to get as many kids to come out to the rally as possible. And it's tough seeing another year go by without being able to give our staff a raise. But when just one person comes to Christ, it's worth it all. We're going to continue to go where few are going: to the schools, to their world.

My only dilemma from the day of fishing? Which was more fun: 10 people becoming believers, or catching those 10 trout? I sure hope you know the answer to that, and the answer to why our team spends over half the year on the road... fishing for men.

"Come, follow me," Jesus said, "and I will send you out to fish for people." Matthew 4:19 (NIV)

PRAYER:

Father, I want to do more than just fish; I want to catch.

CHANGES FOR LOIS

MANY OF YOU KNOW my special needs sister, Lois, or have seen her with me on some of my speaking trips when I've brought her on stage. Lois has lived with our family for the past 11 years since my parents passed away. Our youngest child, Tim, just finished his first year of college. While most people in our situation would be preparing for an empty nest, we came to accept that we would probably never experience that, knowing that Lois would always need care and live with us. It comes with so many joys, and many challenges.

Even though my mom is no longer with us on this earth, I always knew that if our family put Lois in an institution it would qualify as my mom's unforgivable sin.

Two months ago we attended a meeting with Lois' case worker. During the meeting Lois put her head down and said, "Bob, I've got something to tell you." I got a little nervous because I could see she was feeling uncomfortable.

She said, "I don't want to hurt your feelings... but I want to move out."

Did I hear her right? I looked at Carol, then back at Lois, then the caseworker, then back at Lois. I can only imagine the look of shock that must have been on my face. I had to pick my jaw up off the floor. My mind was reeling as I thought, "What in the world? She's 55 years old!"

But Lois continued, "You know Joanne?" (Joanne is her best friend that she grew up with – also a special needs person.) "Her parents just died," Lois said. "And her brothers and sisters think its best if she moves into a house instead of living with them. So her and Julie (another special needs friend) are moving in and asked me to be their roommate."

I sat stunned in disbelief, going through a million reasons in my mind why it couldn't work, and trying to understand what I just heard. But then she said, "Tim always wants to be with his friends and I want to be with my friends, too."

Wow. I knew we had to try and figure out a way to let her try this. I'd feel guilty if we didn't! So, we began doing our homework and met with the other families and the organization that would provide the caregivers. And of course... we prayed.

"God is this you? Is this the loving thing to do? Is this what's best for Lois?"

A week after Lois dropped this bombshell, we got a call from the people who were renting our parent's home, which we still own. It's where we all grew up. The renters had lived there for seven years and we were shocked to hear them say, "We bought a house and will be moving out."

Are you following where this is going? Yep, Lois got to move back into the home where she grew up and lived for more than 40 years, back into her own room!

When she found out she began crying and said, "I get to walk around my old block and live in my old neighborhood? Do you think that anything changed in my room, Bob? And do you think the toilet still leaks?"

I laughed and rejoiced with her at the same time. I don't know how I could have gotten any clearer confirmation. Wow, what a God thing. His timing is amazing.

She's been moved out for a while now, and she loves it. We miss her like crazy, but we still get to pick her and her two friends up for church and visit.

We can't believe it, but we're empty nesters. My wife Carol says that she believes God may be freeing us up to do ministry together in a different way. We've already gone together to some of my speaking engagements, something we were rarely able to do before because someone needed to stay home to care for Lois.

We have a sense that the best years of ministry are still to come. We'll continue to bring hope to youth around the nation, and promote a renewed calling to bring the church back to evangelism and share the gospel with kids before they turn 18.

Lois will always be part of our family and she may even show up on some more stages with me throughout the country. Her life, her story, and the person she is will continue to touch so many, and make it clear that every life is valuable and has purpose, even when we can't understand it.

"We loved you so much that we gave you not only God's Good News but our own lives, too." 1 Thessalonians 2:8

PRAYER

Am I open to change even when it can be hard? Help me to know that when it's you, God, it will bring glory to Your name and continue to advance the Kingdom.

I Like to Be Heard, But No One Can Hear Me...

THERE, IN HER OWN HANDWRITING, it said, "I like to be heard, but no one can hear me."

A 16 year old girl wrote this on a response envelope, also indicating she received Christ. Somehow she related to our stories enough to trust Jesus with her life, including her hurts, pains, disappointments and pressures. And she somehow hoped for more in this life and a life to come in eternity.

This night happened two years after we were contacted by the youth director. He saw me and AJ the Animated Illusionist in Florida at their national youth gathering with 37,000 students. He, along with about 10 students, pledged to bring us into schools in Montana. After 2 years of trying to get the schools to open and raise the funds, we finally performed at both high schools in their city with close to 3,700 students between the two.

Sadly, one of the reasons why the schools finally brought us in is because they had a student who walked into school, went in the bathroom and shot himself in the head. The same school was also just featured on one of the local television news stations because of the problem with bullying. So, needless to say, we walked into some schools with really big issues.

We got two standing ovations, which isn't the norm at public high schools. At the first school, the principal, along with three assistant principals came up to me after the program and said he needed to talk with me. I thought he was going to say there was too much entertainment. Instead, he said we couldn't have hit the nail on the head any more. The reason I mention the concern about too much entertainment is because they had apprehensions about an opening act, fearing it wouldn't have any substance. Yet they said, "Thank you, this is what our school needed."

I spent the next hour talking to students lined up to say thank you and share their stories with me. It ranged from those telling how they were being bullied themselves with tears of pain gushing down their faces, and students who were abused and raped, to a guy who had attempted suicide and is now drinking just to try and fit in for acceptance. There was a guy who said he was the one who would bully others, but now had tears of remorse as he pledged to stop and actually stand up for others.

We drove over thirty hours to get there, missing our families while being on the road once again. But then after just two schools we could only say, "Wow, this doesn't grow old."

Seeing hope come back into the eyes of youth makes the mission as clear and as fresh as always. The passion ignites and the clichés are no longer just hollow words from a brochure, but we really will do *whatever* it takes to reach just one more youth. And all this was just at the high school.

We still got to invite them back at night for a program co-sponsored by the local church. About 1,100 students came out to the rally and we couldn't believe our eyes as the auditorium filled up. AJ got another standing ovation. The kids were so pumped up I wasn't sure they would calm down enough to hear the gospel message, somehow forgetting once again that it's not about us, but only God's spirit can change a heart. So the gospel was seen visually through a sketch by AJ and heard through stories that I told.

In church, we call that preaching. And three hundred, yes, 300 responded to the gospel.

Three hundred, like that girl who wanted so badly to feel heard. Somehow they not only felt heard, but also heard that they were loved. Cases of bibles were given away. Follow up study guides were given to the youth director to start doing discipleship. The church people were spurred on in their faith.

Teen volunteers said things like, "I never thought so and so would come. This was so worth all the work." Then a partnering youth band rocked the house. You could see the student's faces saying with disbelief, "This is all for us?"

A youth worker commented on how the students loved all the entertainment, but how it was much more than entertainment. "We've never had ministry like this here before," he said. "Our evangelism team is praying and so excited to follow up on those who responded."

I personally can't help but think of all the other cities, towns and communities we passed through. How many more youth need to hear this message?

That was just one day. The day prior we were in a town so small that they only had 146 total students from Kindergarten through 12th grade. We did programs at just the Junior and Senior high schools. A group of struggling farmers raised the money to bring us in. They actually got two other schools from surrounding communities to bus their students in. So we got to spread the message of life to 6 schools that day.

At night over 150 people came out to the evening outreach. Over 50 responded to the gospel. This is an area that has been plagued with Meth drug problems to a point where the local jail has posted a sign that says, "Not a Hotel."

As we were trying to teach the students that choices do have consequences, there seemed to be a heavy depression on people just from dealing with everyday life. Like the girl I met whose best friend was in a coma from a car accident, or the guy whose brother died of brain cancer. Then there was the adult who is now on his 3rd marriage, or the guy who felt his future was gone because he became a father at the age of 14.

I was humbled and broken as I, yet again, met a father who melted at the end of the day at the thought of his children hearing a message of hope. I had visited his farm. With a weathered face from years of hard work and worry, he gave us all a hug and said, "Thanks for coming to our community."

As I stood by his combine harvester and looked at the miles and miles of Montana wheat fields, I was reminded how the harvest is plentiful.

Don't stop praying. It's a battle out here. There's work to be done.

PRAYER

The harvest is plentiful, but the workers are few. Father, send more workers.

Confessions of an Evangelist

I HAVE A CONFESSION TO MAKE. I've been critical of the church. As a traveling itinerant evangelist, I have been all over the United States and abroad, and I've fallen into the trap of seeing what's wrong with the church. When I hear that less that 18% of America's youth are in church on a given Sunday,[1] and I hear story after story of people who have walked away from Christ because they've been wounded by the church, it pains my heart and I want to scream, "It's not supposed to be this way!"

I've come across too many people who have never even given Christ a chance because of what they've seen in the lives of church people, or they've seen the church playing politics with their big buildings and sometimes empty words.

I confess I've sometimes wanted to distance myself from the church in an effort to reach people for Christ. As I've looked at history I've found that many others have done the same thing. But as I was taking a walk during some quiet time I was reminded how the Spirit again and again over the years has said to me, "To distance yourself from the church is to distance yourself from me."

The church is His bride, His body, His agent for good in this world. Is she perfect? No. Only Christ is. Are we supposed to pretend and live in denial of the problems? No. But I don't think we're supposed to jump on the wagon with the critics and tear her down even more. No, I refuse. I will not do it.

Life Promotions is a para-church ministry. *Para* means alongside the church – not to take its place, but to work with and be a part of it; to be a ***par***tner to reach the lost.

Picture it this way: We are like a lifeboat on the side of a ship. The church is the ship, a safe place where so many great things are happening. But sometimes it doesn't have the flexibility it needs. So, Life Promotions serves as the lifeboat that is released to go out into a sea of lost people where the church may not be able to navigate as easily, or maneuver as quickly, so that we can bring the lost back to the ship, back to the church. We want to bring youth, first to a saving knowledge of Jesus, and then connect them to the believers who care. That's the church. But we have to work together.

When asked, "What's wrong with the church?" I have to answer the same as G.K. Chesterton did: "I am." If I am part of the church, then I am part of the problem.

But I can also be part of the solution. I can apologize on behalf of the church and let others know that it's a hospital for sinners, not just a museum for saints. I can let others know that we're trying with all our hearts to be like our leader, who is perfect. We'll never arrive, but we'll never stop the pursuit. That's why we're in church: to struggle together, to heal together, to grow together. We have a purpose. We cannot separate ourselves from the church! It's time to start building her up, not tearing her down.

I was so encouraged on a recent speaking trip because I was reminded how what we do on the road would not be possible without the vision of the church to reach into its community. We speak about the value of each life in schools, but when we partner with the local churches to do an evening outreach, we can also share the gospel, and the local church is there to follow up when we leave town. I've been so encouraged by the churches we've worked with recently.

There was a little Baptist church in upstate New York with a congregation that had been gathering for more than 200 years. The building itself was 150 years old. When I walked in I saw beautiful stained glass windows, carved wooden pews, and a pipe organ that filled the front of the church. Along with several other beautiful pieces of furniture, there was a pulpit that alone was over six feet wide. You had to step up into it to see over the top.

But all I could think was, "How are we going to fit a band up on this altar and make it into a stage?"

When we arrived, a meal was being served for the over-60 group, and the people that were helping to put on our event that featured a rock band, with the exception of one couple, were all over 60 themselves. But they graciously allowed us to move the pulpit, and set the drums up behind the communion rail. I usually like to do the rally in a public place because we'll get more people to come to a neutral venue than in a church, but they really wanted it in their sanctuary.

Honestly, we were a bit disappointed with the turnout; only 120 people came. Still the band gave it their all and was jamming out. The bass was booming, the drums were banging, and the lead singer was jumping off the drum set. I caught a glance of the pastor in the back calling someone on the cell phone and I felt a lump in my throat.

"We're in trouble," I thought. "He's calling the district office." I walked up to him, thinking I might need to diffuse a tense situation. But when I approached him, instead of a look of displeasure, I saw a smile on his face. "I'm calling my 20 year old daughter," he said. "She's never going to believe this is happening in our sanctuary. There are more youth here in one night than we've had in the last ten years combined."

Humbled.

I was still disappointed with the turnout, but those hands raised to receive Christ made it all worthwhile. But I was also encouraged by so much more. You see, I was reminded how vital the church is in each community. That night, the kids in that area knew that this church cared. And the kids that did come didn't leave right after the concert – they went downstairs for pizza to be served by the kindest, most loving group of individuals I have met in a long time.

Some of the kids that came may not have had a grandpa or grandma, or parents that cared, but they knew that this unassuming congregation of faithful followers did care. They knew they were loved. They were showered upon with a meal, soda, hugs and pictures with the band in the fellowship hall of the church, a church that was willing to demonstrate His love by putting aside their personal preferences for a greater cause.

All I could think was, "The church is beautiful. The church is his body. I'll defend her with all that I have." It reminded me of these words; the lyrics of a chorus from a song that my nephew, Nate Lenz, wrote. Won't you join me in fighting for the church, and fighting for His Bride?

I'm on Your side, 'cause She's Your Bride
And She's beautiful somewhere deep inside
I'm on Your side, 'cause She's Your Bride
And I'll fight for Her till the day I die
"Ekklesia" by Nate Lenz
Free song download at www.lifedownloads.org

PRAYER

Father, forgive me for those times when I've been critical of your bride. Help me be her defender, and be part of the solution, rather than tearing her down.

Through Victory And Tragedy

IN EARLY DECEMBER a fire destroyed a home, taking the lives of a mom, dad and their son, Charlie – a seventeen year old student from Wautoma High School in Wisconsin. A younger sister was burned so badly that she had to be rushed to Children's Hospital in Milwaukee.

The town was asking, "Where is God now?" Young faith was shaken and others were wrestling with tough questions. The school pulled in counselors and the town rallied around other family survivors and the students. Some concerned Christian parents who wanted to support their students through the grieving process were asking, "What do we do with this crisis of faith?"

They called Life Promotions to see if I could come and speak to the youth to comfort the hurting, but also to try to deal with the questions. But they also wanted youth to be given an opportunity to commit their lives to Christ. Knowing quite a bit about the grieving process, I felt uneasy.

I thought to myself, "It would be a miracle if these youth still believed there even was an all-powerful God after something like this happened. I'll have a hard enough time convincing them that God's not an unloving and uninvolved jerk, let alone expect them to respond to the message of God's grace and commit their lives to follow Him."

I always want to speak. Not this time. I was physically sick for two days and I had more questions than answers myself. I didn't want to come across as insensitive to the grief of family and friends, yet I wanted to be true to scripture and offer the hope and comfort of the gospel. I wrestled to find the balance.

Driving to Wautoma I was still unsettled about what I would say and I called a few friends for prayer. Even after speaking with them I wasn't sure what I would share. What's hard is that so much of my normal presentations use humor, which felt strangely out of place in this circumstance. I normally do prevention work, but this was dealing with the aftermath of a crisis.

When I got there one of the first people I spoke with was Charlie's older sister. "Bob, make sure you tell them that they still need to laugh," she said. "Tell them to remember the good times and the stories about Charlie."

Even though Charlie wasn't a football player himself, the head football coach opened the evening with prayer, affirming with his words, "God is with us in victory, and he is still with us in our tragedy."

See, this football team had recently become state champions for the first time ever. It took lots of hard work, dedication and good coaching. The entire school and town were on cloud nine with an electric excitement over their success.

Teammates encouraged each other with scriptures like Joshua 1:9 "Be strong and courageous. Do not be afraid; do not be discouraged. For the Lord your God will be with you wherever you go." People of faith on the team were like Reggie White in his heyday, pointing one finger to the sky saying, "We're number one," and "All glory to God," simultaneously in one breath.

But the tragedy of Charlie's death shook the town in the midst of their triumph celebrations.

The whole side of the school bleachers was filled as I prepared to speak that night. They had a worship team open with songs of comfort and reflection. I can't even tell you all that I said. But I know I probably offered more questions than answers, and more comfort than challenge. Earlier I had learned that the night before Charlie died he was at a CCD class at the Catholic Church where they played and discussed the song, "I Can Only Imagine" by MercyMe. It's a song about what heaven's going to be like. (This youth group comes to Power of One and Lifest, two music festivals we put on each year. They were introduced to MercyMe and this song at one of our events).

It was only the night before the tragedy that took his life that Charlie imagined what heaven would be like.

I shared the scripture from Matthew 11 that talks about playing a song for you, but you didn't dance. So I encouraged them, "Don't forget the victory. Don't forget the stories and memories of Charlie. It's okay to still have enjoyment in life."

But I went on to share the rest of the scripture from Jesus that tells of playing a dirge (a funeral song) for you, yet you didn't cry. Again, I continued, "God is telling us that it's okay to grieve. Life contains ups and downs. And He is the God that is with you in both." I got to encourage them to not do life without Jesus. As I invited young people to respond, I stood stunned as 150 youth received Christ.

As hands went up everywhere I continued sharing about how we are not meant to do life alone, and how there isn't any one person on the football team who could have won the state championship alone. They were together in victory as a team and they needed each other in this tragedy as well.

I encouraged the youth who received Christ to come down to the middle of the gymnasium to grieve together and to acknowledge that Christ is still there in the midst. As more than a hundred students flooded the gymnasium floor, I then invited their parents and friends and others to gather around them just like they did for a victory in the football championship. The bleachers emptied and everyone was on the gymnasium floor.

It was one of the most moving experiences I've had in all my years of ministry. We ended by saying the Lord's Prayer together. As a perfect cap to the evening, the worship team led us in the song, "I Can Only Imagine." You could feel the presence of Jesus in the midst of the pain, yet bringing hope through one another. I encouraged them to share hugs and stories and pray with each other, and an hour and a half later people were still there.

What a God. What a community.

Remember... "Be strong and courageous. Do not be afraid; do not be discouraged, for the LORD your God will be with you wherever you go." Joshua 1:9 (NIV)

Through both victory and tragedy.

PRAYER

Allow me to be real with people like you were real with people, to weep with those who weep and mourn with those who mourn. Forgive me for the times when I've put on a mask and pretended to not be fazed by the struggles of life around me.

Only in Alaska

OUR FLIGHT WAS CANCELLED because of a blizzard that was dumping four feet of snow in the area. We were in the Anchorage airport waiting for our flight to Valdez, Alaska. We were disappointed that we would miss our school programs and rally, and wondered how long we'd be stranded.

"Why don't you just drive instead?"

What?! These were the words of our local sponsor who helped bring us into the area. Only in Alaska could you get 4 feet of snow and still have the local residents think we wouldn't have any problems driving.

So, you guessed it... we drove. It took 6 hours to drive through the mountain pass. There were many close calls where we almost got stuck. It brought back memories of when I was in North Carolina and they canceled school where I was supposed to speak because of a half inch of snow.

Yet another day on this trip we were once again in an airport waiting to pick up our luggage at baggage claim. Like in many airports, there was a wall of windows overlooking a sidewalk outside. As we watched passers-by outside, we couldn't believe our eyes. Unlike many airports, along with passing cars and pedestrians who didn't even seem to notice, there walked a large bull moose on the sidewalk, casually weaving in and out of traffic. I'm not sure if the moose was looking for his luggage or what.

While in Alaska, I heard a new term I hadn't heard before called "Couch Surfing." While speaking at an alternative school I found out that a couch surfer is a high school student who is homeless but is still trying to go to school to get their diploma. They end up going from one friend's house to another, sleeping on their couches.

High school years are hard enough. I don't know how they do it being homeless as well. It seems so difficult to believe it's possible to be homeless in Alaska through the winter. But this is reality for many. In fact, I learned that two homeless men I met last year when I was in Nome, Alaska, froze to death, and another lost his leg because of frostbite.

I wasn't sure how to gauge one particular assembly program we did because the response from students didn't seem as enthusiastic as usual. Jokes and funny stories received very few laughs, and the kids hardly seemed to respond or clap with the band. I thought that perhaps they were just tired because it was the first thing in the morning, or maybe they missed the surf and spent the night out on the streets in an Alaskan winter.

Despite the unenthusiastic group earlier in the day, I felt good about the rally that evening where many youth responded to the gospel. After the rally I met a girl named Angel. It was then that I found out she had attempted suicide the night before. She had attended my school assembly program earlier in the day, hiding the cuts on her wrist with a myriad of band aids and bracelets. After the school program that I thought had such little impact, Angel turned herself in to the counselor at the school to seek help.

When I saw her that night she had gauze on both wrists instead of all the bracelets. She was a tall and attractive girl who looked more like 30 than 17. She sat in the second row for the rally. This time she did laugh at the stories. Afterwards, she told me she was moved by my talk and felt hope for the first time in a long time.

I couldn't help but notice that she hadn't responded to the gospel, so I hoped maybe she had Christianity in her background. But after our discussion I found out she was heavily involved in Wicca, a pagan religion.

Instead of passing judgment on her, I explored why. She told me one of the reasons was because the Wiccan religion has female goddesses. You see, she had been abused and assaulted by men who, in name, used the "Christian" title.

My heart sunk. Their hypocrisy had repelled her from the Christian faith.

She said, "I loved everything you said but I'm not into Jesus." I replied, "If you're not into Jesus then why did you come tonight and why are you talking to me?"

"Because," she continued, "At the school the person that introduced you said people had donated money for you to come. If people who I don't even know care about me enough to have a speaker come and they really believed that you were genuine and believed in what you were talking about, then maybe there was some hope for me."

She softened as she spoke the next words, "You really encouraged me with what you said."

For a moment I was taken aback. Despite her pain, she came. I couldn't help but apologize for ways in which the church, or people who call themselves Christians, have hurt women or pushed down their dignity in the name of Christianity. "That's so not how our leader Jesus treated women," I said.

I told her the story of the woman at the well, whom the world had used and abused and left to feel worthless – the woman who even made bad choices herself. I shared how Jesus broke all customs and social barriers to reach out to her with worth, value and forgiveness. "If you like anything that I said tonight," I continued. "I want you to know that I get it all from that person, Jesus."

I wish I could put a nice bow on this story and tell you that Angel responded to the gospel that night. That didn't happen. But Angel now has a seed of hope and a taste of the real Jesus because of those who helped us go there. She said it herself, "If people who I don't even know care about me enough to have a speaker come... then maybe there's some hope for me."

You care. And there is hope. Angel now believes that.

PRAYER

Forgive us for how we, the church, have hurt others and made others to feel inferior in the name of Jesus.

Love – No Disclaimers

I CAN'T STOP CRYING. I can't stop hurting. It's like I feel what they're feeling, and I sense the hopelessness of their questions, "Why not just die? Why not just end it all?"

There are some days when I feel the pain of the kids that I speak to more than others. Today is one of those days. I just finished an assembly program with 400 junior high students where I talked about bullying and showing respect. A boy that is in a special needs class came up to me afterwards and started sharing about how others call him retarded and make fun of him. He shared about a class that he said would probably be his favorite, but he hates going because he feels so bad about himself when people make fun of him and put him down.

Then a sharp-looking red-headed kid with freckles all over his face came up to me. I imagined that he should have had the bubbly joy of my red-headed daughter Joyel, but instead I saw pain in his eyes. The pain reminded me of a victim of war, which wasn't far from reality for him. People ridiculed and laughed at him, calling him a faggot bastard. While waiting at the bus stop, kids would throw rocks and make fun of him. He feels like he's all alone.

"What do I do," he asked? "How do I deal with it when they call me these names?"

All I could wonder is, "Where are the followers of Jesus that will stand up for the least of these? Who is there to love, encourage, and tell him he's been made in the image of God? Who is there to give him hope?"

Then a senior in high school came up to me. I was surprised to see a high school student among all these junior high kids. It turned out he was there because he was tutoring a class for 6th graders. He began crying. "I didn't expect to come to an assembly program today," he said, "but it's what I needed so bad."

Tears streamed down his face as he began crying uncontrollably with snot coming from his nose. "I had a horrible weekend," he continued. "Six of the jocks in school followed me to my car and called me names and kept saying I was gay, and they beat me up." My heart sank as I watched his pain-filled face. "But the worst thing was when no one would even stop the junior high kid from spitting on me."

No one. No one. No one deserves to be treated like this! May the people of faith be the ones that are leading the way to seek out opportunities to love, to understand, to invite, to care, to defend, and to stand for justice.

Real righteousness is found when you care for the dignity of every person, even the person you disagree with.

The principal came up after witnessing those three kids talking with me. "I can't believe you held the attention of 400 students for 45 minutes," he said. "They laughed and cried and absorbed every word you said. But to have them trust you so much to share these deep stories – that says a lot. This is a gift back to you, showing the difference you're making. Thank you. This is exactly what our school needed."

He continued to tell me there are three things the school is trying to teach students: respect for themselves, respect for others, and respect for property. "You hit every single one," he said. "It's like you designed this talk for our school, and we want to get you in every school possible."

"Great," I thought. "Let's make it happen." But I couldn't get my mind off the kids who just poured their hearts out to me. Honestly, it pains my heart that we have allowed some of the struggles that these kids are dealing with to become an issue to debate, instead of loving people.

No matter what stance you feel you need to take on an issue, God has commanded us to love others. There are no disclaimers. May we be known for whom we follow, more than known for whom we fight.

God forbid that we allow some of the struggles that these kids are facing to become a political platform, a theological issue to be debated, or something that we want to protest and picket. Because in the meantime, kids are struggling with their value and worth as others who are fueled by self-righteousness treat them as sub-human. And we silently stand by.

PRAYER

God help us to stand up for the value of every person.

A Thank You. A Gut Ache. A Call.

I'M SURE YOU'VE WATCHED THE NEWS and have seen soldiers returning home from active duty. The reunion scene of a husband with his wife and children or other loved ones brings a lump to your throat. No words can capture the moment. You're flooded with feelings of relief and mutual gratitude.

Home.

You see the sacrifice, not just of the soldier, but of the whole family and the bigger team.

I just came back from a three month sabbatical, a time to refresh, write and study after 29 years of service in the ministry. My heart is overflowing with gratitude. When I began my sabbatical it was very clear that it was as much for my wife, Carol, as it was for me. She has been the one with all the added responsibilities at home while I've been on the road half the year. This time of refreshment with

Jesus was so needed and made only more special because of the time spent with Carol.

We also had time with kids and other family like never before. We even went to a hotel for a weekend. The reality of my time away struck my heart when one of my kids said, "I think this is the first time we've ever been at a hotel together where you weren't scheduled to speak." The timing of our time off was perfect as we got to experience our daughter, Danielle, making us grandparents.

Life is so good.

The last three months are like none I've ever experienced in 28 years of marriage and ministry... a sense of peace my heart has never tasted.

I came back to the office and set up meetings with the different departments: speaking team, festival team and the development team. It was so cool to see the line-up for Lifest, the music festival we put on each summer in Oshkosh, WI, and also to see the full calendar for myself and Life Promotions' other speakers in the coming months.

But then our speaking team began sharing the situations of some of the schools where I was scheduled to speak. The first school on the East Coast had a suicide in November and another student death from a car crash only a month later. They wanted me to know that the school is really hurting, and want me to help them deal with the loss.

For the next school, they wanted me to address the bullying problem. It has been so bad that if a student raises his hand to offer an answer, they'll not only call him teacher's pet, but stab him in the back with pens.

The school after that was in British Columbia Canada where two girls got into a fight. One of them had a knife, and when the fight ended, the other girl was dead. The community is devastated and hoping that with AJ the Animated Illusionist and I coming there, it will bring reconciliation and hope for the future.

A suicide death, accidental death, bullying and a murder. All of this, plus schools are having their budgets slashed, and some also expressed warnings over their concerns about the separation of church and state.

The peace inside disappeared and was replaced with a gut ache. A knot in my stomach. A pain in my heart pierced with such heaviness it brought me to tears and almost depression. I know something has to be done for these students, but in an instant I felt overwhelmed again, inadequate and insecure.

I walked into another meeting with my development team to find out that we've lost some monthly supporters because of the economy. My heart hurts for these faithful givers, some who are experiencing layoffs and financial distress. And as the president of the organization, I felt the pressure to provide financially.

Can I be candidly honest? I didn't want to be deployed back again onto the front lines. I think I'd rather be a civilian instead of in full-time service. I would rather not leave my wife, home, family and friends. I'd prefer not to be under attack by the enemy and the fire of scrutiny from other believers.

When I got home that night I shared my feelings with my son, Tim. He saw my struggle and could sense my reluctance to return to a leadership role, and to the cultural and spiritual warfare going on in the hearts of our nation's youth.

Tim tried to cheer me on. Hitting me on my shoulder, he said, "Come on dad, fire up, you can do it!" I felt like a lineman on his football team receiving a pep talk, facing fourth and goal. But nothing he tried worked.

Then the moment stilled. He got really quiet, looked me in the eye and said, "Dad, it's your calling."

Tears filled my eyes. My son had spoken truth. It's what God has designed me for.

So, as I pen this I'm headed onto another airplane to return to the front lines again as an act of obedience to our God, to answer the call. And as I go I'm convinced of this more than ever: God's heart is still for every one of these youth.

"...a great door for effective work has opened to me, and there are many who oppose me." 1 Corinthians 16:9 (NIV)

PRAYER

Thank you that I'm not alone in my service to You, whatever my role or calling is in Your Kingdom. Make me part of a greater team that will stand up together against the enemy.

End Notes

I Lost a Junior High Kid

1. The American Church Research Project, By David T. Olson (2008) www.theamericanchurch.org
2. The Barna Group Ltd., *Evangelism is Most Effective Among Kids*, (2004) www.barna.org

I Never Wanted to Be "*That Guy*"

1. Gallup Polling, *Americans' Church Attendance Inches Up in 2010*, (June 25, 2010) www.gallup.com
2. National Church Life Survey, *Church Attendance as a Percentage of the Australian Population*, (2001) www.ncls.org.au

It's Urgent

1. The Barna Group Ltd., *Evangelism is Most Effective Among Kids*, (2004) www.barna.org

Confessions of an Evangelist

1. The American Church Research Project, By David T. Olson (2008) www.theamericanchurch.org

About Life Promotions

At Life Promotions we reach over half a million young people across the nation each year with the hope of the gospel. Founder and president, Bob Lenz, has an intense passion to bring hope and lasting change to hurting youth, and offers heartfelt messages that help them deal with real life.

With 2 out of 3 people coming to faith before the age of 18, it is our mission to reach as many young people as possible with the message of grace, hope and love. In addition to founder, Bob Lenz, additional speakers help further our mission and multiply the efforts being made.

FAITH-BASED PROGRAMS

- Partnering with local churches to host Christian outreaches open to the entire community
- Offering free bibles and study guides to those who respond to the gospel
- Equipping local pastors to provide personal follow-up with each student

SCHOOL ASSEMBLY PROGRAMS

- Poignant, funny, touching, and most importantly... effective
- Value-based presentations: Bully & suicide prevention, self-image, value and respect
- Encouraging student leaders of today to continue on the path of being leaders tomorrow

FESTIVALS

- Lifest – one of the nation's largest Christian music festivals, held each July in Oshkosh, WI, featuring more than 100 top-name Christian artists, speakers and comedians, plus camping, food and activities. Information at Lifest.com.
- Power of One – a one-day festival held each fall, featuring national musicians, speakers and workshops, focused on bringing youth of all denominations together for a day of Christian teaching, fellowship, music and personal growth. Information at PowerOfOneOnline.com

To learn more, to get involved, or to receive booking information on having Bob Lenz speak at your next event, please contact us.

<18> INSTILLING HOPE IN YOUTH

Lifepromotions.com

800-955-LIFE

Proceeds from the sale of this book go to further Life Promotions' mission of instilling hope in youth by sharing the love of Jesus. There are more stories waiting to be written about the lives of young people still needing to be reached.